ARNOLD SCHWARZENEGGER

BY
B. S. WATSON

kidsbooks®
Incorporated

Copyright © 1992 Kidsbooks, Inc.
7004 North Carolina Avenue
Chicago, IL 60645

ISBN: 1-56156-063-4

Manufactured in the United States of America

TABLE OF CONTENTS

Page

Introduction

It's not often that the classic American dream of rags to riches actually comes true. It's not often that a person reaches the top of one career, let alone two, before the age of 45. And it's not often that an unknown arrives in America and winds up marrying into one of its most famous families.

But for Arnold Schwarzenegger all of these dreams have come true. Born into a poor family in Austria, Arnold now earns over 10 million dollars per movie. He was the youngest bodybuilder to ever win the coveted Mr. Universe contest, doing so in 1967 at the age of 20! He holds every record there is in the field of bodybuilding, having won seven Mr. Olympia contests and five Mr. Universe titles, including an astounding three titles in one year, 1970, when he won the Mr. Universe, Mr. Olympia, and Pro Mr. World contests!

Having conquered the bodybuilding world, Arnold took the world of movie acting by storm.

He is now one of the movie business' top box office stars and stays on top of the movie world year after year.

When he is not working out or making hit movies, Arnold serves as chairman of the President's Council on Physical Fitness, tirelessly touring the country, speaking to adults and children alike about the value of staying in shape.

And, as if all these accomplishments were not enough, on April 26, 1986 Arnold Schwarzenegger married CBS Morning News reporter Maria Shriver, the niece of the late president John F. Kennedy. It was one of the most highly-publicized weddings of all time. A handsome rags-to-riches celebrity movie star, who also happened to be the greatest bodybuilder ever, marrying the beautiful television journalist, who just happened to be part of one of the most famous families in American history!

But this storybook saga has very humble beginnings. Arnold Schwarzenegger was not always rich and famous—quite the opposite. It's taken many years of very hard work and rugged determination to bring this champion and celebrity to his place in the world of sports and entertainment.

To find the beginning of Arnold's story, we must travel many thousands of miles from the glamorous Schwarzenegger mansion in Pacific Palisades, California, to a small mountain village in the European country of Austria.

Arnold Schwarzenegger: Superstar of the 90s.

Arnold pumps up.

Chapter 1

ARNOLD IN AUSTRIA

Arnold Schwarzenegger was born on July 30, 1947 in the village of Thal, Austria. This charming village was just on the outskirts of a fairly large city called Graz. Although the scenery in Thal was breathtaking, many of its residents, including the Schwarzeneggers, were quite poor.

Arnold's parents, Gustav and Aurelia, moved to Thal when Gustav was named chief of police of the small village. Gustav was also a talented musician who played six instruments, but as head of the Schwarzenegger household, he was very strict. A former soldier in World War II, he ran his home like a military commander. This made things hard on young Arnold and his older brother, Meinhard.

"My brother and I used to have to get up at six every morning and do chores before we went to school," recalls Arnold. "After school, we came straight home to do more work around the house."

The house Arnold grew up in had no indoor plumbing or central heating system. Life was certainly tough for this future superstar. Very few people had cars or phones, and the only way to get to the nearby city of Graz was to walk many miles. Arnold's tough years as a child helped prepare him for challenges later in life.

"My father really shaped Meinhard and me," says Arnold. "If I wanted anything, my father told me to go out and work for it. I hated the hard work, but I learned that if I worked hard enough, I could have anything I wanted."

Gustav was very difficult to please, and sometimes Arnold was afraid of his father. "He acted like a general," remembers Arnold. "He checked to see that I was eating the right things, that I did my homework on time, and that my clothes were clean and neat."

But if Gustav was a tough taskmaster, he was also a dedicated teacher. Every week, he would teach his boys about art and music. On Sundays they would walk around the countryside, as Gustav lectured about nature. Sometimes they went to see plays or concerts. Occasionally Arnold would go to hear his father play in the police department band.

Like most wives in Austria in the 1950s, Aurelia took care of the house—cooking, cleaning, even carrying buckets of water in from outside. "My mother was a very neat and tidy person," recalls Arnold. "Everything always sparkled in our house. I'm that way now, because of her."

It might surprise you when you look at Arnold today, but as a child, he was small and often sick. As he grew, Gustav encouraged Arnold to try different sports, as a way to build himself up physically, and also to give him self-confidence.

"I always dreamed of becoming a champion," says Arnold. "I wasn't sure which sport it would be, but becoming the best at what I did was very important to me."

To achieve this goal Arnold tried many sports, including skiing, ice curling, and soccer. The more he played, the healthier and stronger he grew. By the time he was 12, Arnold was playing on the best soccer team in Graz.

In addition to sports, Arnold loved going to the movies. When he was six, his father took him into Graz to see the former Olympic swimmer turned Hollywood actor, Johnny Weismuller, who was in Austria for the opening of a new swimming pool. Arnold was immediately star struck.

Whenever he could, he took the long hike into Graz and snuck into the movies. Sitting in a movie theater in Graz, Austria, 13-year-old Arnold Schwarzenegger watched American movie stars like Steve Reeves, who starred in a series of

11

Hercules movies; Johnny Weismuller, who starred in a series of Tarzan movies; and John Wayne, star of countless cowboy and soldier movies—all larger than life heroes. Who would have dreamed that one day Arnold himself would be up on the big screen, starring as the hero!

In addition to tales of heroics and adventure, American movies provided Arnold with something else—a vision of the promised land called America.

"I loved watching movies about big cities in America—Chicago, New York, Los Angeles. I was fascinated by the size of these places, and by the size of the country as well. Somehow I knew that I had to see this place, and that my destiny was tied up with the USA."

The road to America, and his eventual success, began when Arnold was 14. That summer, Kurt Marnul, Mr. Austria, the most celebrated bodybuilder in the country, opened a training gym in Graz.

Arnold began to work out there as a way to make his legs stronger for soccer playing, but quickly fell in love with bodybuilding itself.

Arnold quit playing soccer and began to work out as often as he could. He would spend six days a week at the training gym in Graz, lifting weights and doing repetitions, until his muscles began to grow.

At the same time, Arnold began buying and reading all the American bodybuilding magazines he could find. He became totally obsessed with all aspects of the sport.

Arnold knew that he had found the thing that would someday make him the champion he always knew he would be!

"I knew that bodybuilding was my ticket to freedom," recalls Arnold. "It was a way out of Austria, and a way to break free from my strict father. The choice to become a bodybuilder was the first decision I ever made on my own, without consulting my parents. I was on my way to becoming my own person, to becoming a man!"

Arnold was on his way to a lot more than that!

Arnold is a bodybuilding champion.

Chapter 2

PUMPING IRON

Bodybuilding has been around since the time of the ancient Greeks, though it began its rise to current popularity in the late 1800s in Europe. In the 1940s the sport became popular in Venice, California on a beach that became known as "Muscle Beach." By the 1960s, when Arnold Schwarzenegger got involved, bodybuilding was an internationally known and respected competitive sport.

Bodybuilding requires endless hours of hard work and discipline. Arnold's difficult upbringing and will to be a champion gave him the tools needed to be successful at this grueling, demanding sport.

Setting goals for himself has always been a big part of Arnold's life. The goal he set for himself as a bodybuilder was a huge one. Arnold wanted to become Mr. Universe!

Each year the Mr. Universe contest was held among the world's top bodybuilders. The winner of this coveted title could then go on to compete for the title of Mr. Olympia—the highest honor in the world for a bodybuilder.

Arnold entered his first competition at the age of 17, in 1964. Although he didn't win the contest, he enjoyed the taste of competition, and vowed to win next time. But before Arnold actually won his first bodybuilding contest, he was to earn other athletic honors.

Ice curling is a sport popular in many European countries and Austria is no exception. It's played by sliding an iron disk across ice, toward a circle some distance away, similar to the game of shuffleboard.

In between training for bodybuilding contests, Arnold managed to find time to become the Austrian and then the European Junior Ice Curling Champion!

This pleased Arnold, but he never lost sight of his true goal—to win a bodybuilding competition. This would first happen for him in 1965. That year, Arnold won the Junior Mr. Europe title. It was a start, but Arnold felt that he still had a long way to go.

Shortly after winning his first title, Arnold moved to Munich, Germany, where he began to train at Putziger's Gym, the top bodybuilding gym in Germany. This hard work paid off the following year when Arnold won his first major bodybuilding competition, the Mr. Germany contest. Arnold was on his way, and the bodybuilding world was beginning to take notice of this young marvel.

After months in Germany of training for up to seven hours a day, Arnold was ready for his first major international contest, the 1966 Mr. Universe contest. This contest was held in London, England.

When Arnold arrived in London for the contest, he met, for the first time, bodybuilders from all over the world, including the American bodybuilders whom he idolized. Arnold was amazed at how professionally these Americans presented themselves. They had more than just big muscles. These men gave off poise and confidence on stage. Their bodies were tanned, their poses were perfect. They were the ultimate in class.

Arnold came in second in the 1966 Mr. Universe contest, but he was far from disappointed. Finishing second for someone so young— he was only 19—was certainly a major accomplishment. In addition, Arnold learned a great deal from his experience of spending time with the American bodybuilders. This only made him look forward more to next year's contest, and beyond that to the day when he would finally go to America.

His hard work during the next year really paid off. In 1967, Arnold Schwarzenegger became the youngest man ever to win the Mr. Universe contest. At the age of 20, the poor kid from Thal was on top of the bodybuilding world!

The year 1968 brought Arnold not only his second Mr. Universe title, but also the realization of his lifelong dream. He finally came to the land he had only seen in the movies, America!

Joe Weider, the world's largest publisher of bodybuilding magazines at that time, took a liking to Arnold after seeing him win the Mr. Universe title in 1967. Weider invited Arnold to come to the USA to continue his training and to write bodybuilding articles for Weider's magazines.

Arnold packed his bags and flew to America, the land of his dreams. But dreams don't always turn out the way you plan. At least not at first. "My desire, which I was sure I could accomplish, was to train in America, and beat all Americans in a contest held in their country," says Arnold.

Arnold was wrong. He lost the Mr. Universe contest held in Miami, Florida to an American bodybuilder. The weeks after the contest were among the hardest of his entire life. He was lonely in America, he had trouble reading and speaking English, and he found it very tough to make friends. Joe Weider came to the rescue.

Weider brought Arnold out to California. He gave him a car, a place to live, a place to train, and a regular salary. In return, Arnold wrote articles for Weider's bodybuilding magazines, gave advice to young bodybuilders, and endorsed fitness products that Weider was trying to promote.

Soon Arnold was happy again. He loved the California lifestyle, the warm weather, and the many beaches. Arnold responded by training harder than ever before.

Soon Arnold was back in competitions, winning his third, fourth, and fifth Mr. Universe titles. In 1970 Arnold Schwarzenegger did something that no other bodybuilder had ever done. He won the top three contests—Mr. Olympia, Mr. Universe, and Pro Mr. World—all in the same year! He had broken new ground in the sport, and was now the most famous bodybuilder of all time.

At the height of his bodybuilding success, another of Arnold's lifelong dreams came true. He got the chance to act in a movie.

Arnold Schwarzenegger — coming soon to a theater near you

Chapter 3

THE EARLY MOVIES

By 1970 Arnold had become such an internationally known celebrity that it should have come as no surprise when the movie world took notice of him. His amazing physique, dark good looks, and dynamic personality made him a natural for the silver screen. His first role, however, was in a movie shot for the small screen.

Arnold's first film, *Hercules Goes Bananas* (sometimes called *Hercules Goes to New York*), was not an award-winning film. But when the chance to act was offered to Arnold he simply could not refuse. Not only was it a chance to appear in a film, but it was a Hercules film, just like the ones starring Steve Reeves that Arnold watched as a boy back in Austria.

The producers of the film were uncomfortable with Arnold's difficult last name, so for his movie debut, he appeared as "Arnold Strong."

Although the movie got terrible reviews, Arnold had fallen in love with acting, as he had done with bodybuilding years before. This young man who had built his life by setting goals, set a new goal for himself—to become a big Hollywood movie star.

Arnold took the money he made from *Hercules Goes Bananas* and used it to continue his lifelong quest to improve himself. He invested in real estate, something that continues to be a big money maker for Arnold today. He also started taking classes at night. He learned how to speak and write English properly—tools he knew that he would need to be a success in Hollywood. Arnold eventually got a degree in business and economics.

Arnold's second acting appearance was in a real feature film. In 1973 an actor friend of Arnold's named David Arkin, told movie director Robert Altman about Arnold. Altman was casting a film called *The Long Good-bye*, a movie based on the Raymond Chandler novel, starring Elliot Gould as Chandler's famous detective, Philip Marlowe.

Altman was looking for a big, tough-looking guy to play a hoodlum. It was a small part—Arnold just stood there without saying a word, looking big and mean. But for Arnold it was a chance to appear in a major feature film, directed by one of Hollywood's top directors. The movie was released in 1974.

Arnold's next break came when he made an appearance on *The Merv Griffin Show*, a popular television talk show. Arnold was on to speak about bodybuilding. The great comedienne Lucille Ball just happened to see the show, and was struck by Arnold's charm and wit. Lucy phoned Arnold and invited him to appear with her on her upcoming TV special called *Happy Anniversary and Good-bye*, co-starring Art Carney. Lucy arranged for Arnold to take acting lessons before his appearance.

Arnold applied the acting lessons Lucy provided to his next film project. Director Bob Rafelson, fresh off of his success with the film *Five Easy Pieces*, needed an actor to play the part of a bodybuilder named Joe Santo in his upcoming film *Stay Hungry*.

The author of the book *Stay Hungry*, Charles Gaines, arranged a meeting between Arnold and Rafelson. Arnold got the part. He loved playing a bodybuilder. In the movie he falls in love with the woman who runs the gym where he trains. This part was played by Sally Fields. Jeff Bridges also starred in the movie, which was released in 1976.

"He worked so hard on the details," recalls director Rafelson. "One scene called for Joe Santo to play the fiddle. Arnold practiced the movement of playing so much that when we finally filmed it, it looked like he was really playing the fiddle!"

Arnold was starting to work with some of Hollywood's top actors and directors. Major success was just around the corner for him. But during this exciting time, tragedy struck twice within two years.

In May of 1971, Arnold's older brother, Meinhard, died in a car accident. In December of 1972, Arnold's father, Gustav, died of a stroke. These were painful deaths for Arnold, and he was very saddened by the loss of his family.

Arnold coped with the sadness by pushing himself to work even harder on his movie career. Big success in the movies would happen for Arnold in 1977, but the path to that success began back in 1972.

In September of that year, Arnold met a photographer named George Butler at the Mr. America contest. From the moment they met, Butler was fascinated by Arnold. "It was clear to me that Arnold was a star," recalls Butler. "His presence was just incredible."

Butler was working with author Charles Gaines (the man who wrote *Stay Hungry*) on a book about the world of bodybuilding, to be called *Pumping Iron*. When Butler met Arnold, he convinced Gaines to make Arnold the focus of the book. Gaines and Schwarzenegger soon became fast friends.

Pumping Iron was published in 1974. It only served to increase Arnold's exposure and popularity outside the world of bodybuilding.

In 1975 it was decided that *Pumping Iron* would be made into a movie. Arnold was asked to play himself in the starring role of this documentary film. Ironically, the role of playing himself as a bodybuilder would be the role that made him a huge movie star.

Filming on *Pumping Iron* began in June of 1975. Arnold worked harder on this film than on any of the others that came before it. He returned to intensive acting lessons with Jack Nicholson's acting teacher, Eric Morris.

In November of 1975 Arnold won his sixth Mr. Olympia contest. His victory was captured on film and is part of *Pumping Iron*. Following this victory, Arnold shocked the bodybuilding world by announcing his retirement from competition. The man who rewrote the book on competitive bodybuilding would compete no more. Arnold decided to concentrate on making movies and running his many business ventures.

In January of 1977 *Pumping Iron* opened with a gala bash at New York's Plaza Theater. Arnold flew his mother, Aurelia, in from Austria for the occasion. It was Arnold's evening, and Arnold's movie.

Audiences saw Arnold training, kidding around, talking about bodybuilding, and competing in contests. They also got to learn about Arnold's difficult childhood and his life in Austria.

The movie was a big hit, fans all around the world fell in love with the charismatic Austrian, and Arnold became a major celebrity.

Arnold took some time off after the release of *Pumping Iron*. It was during this vacation that Arnold met Maria Shriver, niece of the late President John F. Kennedy. They hit it off right away, and began dating. It was a courtship that would last for nearly ten years.

Arnold was never one to take it easy for very long, and so following a brief break he got right back into making movies. Unfortunately, roles as perfect as the one in *Pumping Iron* don't come along every day. Arnold's next three films were not well received by the critics or movie fans.

The Villain saw Arnold in a small role as a shy cowboy. Although he was happy to work with Hollywood legends Kirk Douglas and Ann Margaret, he was quite upset when the film disappeared from theaters quickly.

A television appearance on *The Streets of San Francisco* followed, as did a meeting with film producer Dino De Laurentiis. Arnold had heard that De Laurentiis was planning to do a movie based on the comic book hero Flash Gordon. Arnold wanted the part, but didn't hit if off with De Laurentiis at their initial meeting.

Instead, Arnold ended up playing another bodybuilder for his next role. He played the part of

Mickey Hargitay in a TV movie called *The Jayne Mansfield Story*, which appeared in 1979.

That same year he appeared in an unsuccessful comedy called *The Scavenger Hunt*. Both of these films bombed, causing Arnold to begin to worry about his acting career.

Arnold was smart enough to know that he next needed to chose a role that would be suited to his personality and physical powers. He found that role in the person of a pulp fiction and comic book hero whom he had loved and read about for many years. It was a fictional hero who lived 12,000 years ago!

Arnold is Conan!

Chapter 4

ARNOLD IN ACTION: CONAN AND BEYOND

Conan the Barbarian lived in the pages of the pulp fiction series of books written by Robert E. Howard, and later in a series of comic book adventures. Arnold devoured each story, and when word got out that a Conan movie was going to be made, Arnold was determined that he would be the actor to bring the character to life on the big screen.

He knew some of the people involved in the project, and so he felt confident that he would have no trouble getting the part. Then he found out that Dino De Laurentiis was producing the movie. De Laurentiis said that he wanted a big-name actor for the part of Conan, and he refused to use Arnold.

Fortunately for Arnold, the film's director, John Milius was a very big Schwarzenegger fan. He wanted Arnold for the role, and he managed to convince De Laurentiis to use Arnold. "Arnold was the world's best-built man," explains director Milius. "I told De Laurentiis that if we didn't use him we would have to get someone to make a replica of Arnold, using makeup and false muscles. Why fake it when you have the real thing right here!"

De Laurentiis saw the point, and by the time Arnold showed up on the set to begin filming, the producer greeted the star by saying "Schwarzenegger, you *are* Conan!" Arnold was very flattered. De Laurentiis even bought Arnold a full set of bodybuilding equipment to use during the filming on location in Spain.

As much as Arnold was perfect for the role, it proved to be the most grueling work of his life. Even months before shooting started, Arnold not only trained as hard as he ever did for a bodybuilding competition, but he took lessons in sword fighting, rope climbing, and horseback riding—all skills of which Conan was a master. Insisting on doing all his own stunts in the film, Arnold needed to convince the audience that these skills were second nature to him as well.

Once shooting began, the set in Spain was freezing cold. Other locations proved to be blazingly hot or filled with mosquitoes. During the course of shooting, Arnold was run over by horses, bitten by a camel, attacked by wolves, and cut by an axe! He went to extremes to make Conan look real.

Arnold's pain and hard work paid off. *Conan the Barbarian* was the hit action movie of the summer of 1982, bringing in more than $100 million worldwide. Arnold was a hit in his first mainstream starring role, and almost immediately talk of a sequel began.

Work on the sequel, *Conan the Destroyer*, was scheduled to begin in late 1983. But before Arnold reported to the set, he had one very important piece of business to take care of.

On September 16, 1983, at the Shrine Auditorium in Los Angeles, Arnold Schwarzenegger became an American citizen. Wearing a red, white, and blue suit and a red tie, Arnold proclaimed, "I always believed in shooting for the top, and becoming an American is like becoming a member of the winning team."

Soon after getting his citizenship Arnold went to Mexico to start shooting *Conan the Destroyer*. His work on the sequel was not quite as grueling as the original, although he still had to follow a tough regimen.

"I spent at least two hours a day working out," said Arnold. "That's a lot when you are working on a film, and you need to be ready for the cameras all day long. But I had to look good for the Conan fight scenes, so I made the time for working out."

Conan the Destroyer opened in 1984. By that time Arnold had a huge number of fans who anxiously awaited the release of each of his

Arnold is proud to be an American citizen.

movies. The fans loved the new Conan film, even if the critics did not.

The following year, Arnold would make his most successful film so far. *The Terminator* not only made more money than any of his previous films, but it marked the first time that Arnold received rave reviews from the critics for his acting. He was named International Star of the Year for 1984, and the critics not only praised Arnold's acting, but they put *The Terminator* onto many of their Top Ten lists of the best movies of the year.

The Terminator marked a change of character for Arnold. It was the first time that he played the bad guy in a movie. "Because of the Conan movies and my talks about fitness and my work with bodybuilding, I have this image of being the good guy," explains Arnold. "I was a bit concerned about how audiences would accept me playing a ruthless robot!"

Arnold really enjoyed the challenge of playing the bad guy, and he didn't need to worry about audiences accepting him. "It was really funny," he recalls. "I would go to theaters to watch the movie with audiences, and three quarters of the way through, people started cheering. They were actually rooting for the bad guy, just because it was me!"

While the physical routine of making *The Terminator* was not as grueling as it was during the Conan movies, Arnold had to sit in a chair

Arnold rescues his daughter in *Commando*.

for hours each day while the makeup people turned him into the deadly robot that he played. His trademark line "I'll be back," has made its way into the language of American pop culture. In every possible way, *The Terminator* was a smash hit.

Following the success of *The Terminator*, Arnold picked up his sword and animal skins once again, in 1985, co-starring with Brigitte Nielsen in the Conan-like adventure *Red Sonja*. Nielsen played a female superhero from the same time period as Conan. It featured great sword fighting battle scenes, and Schwarzenegger fans got to see their hero in action again as a mythical warrior from thousands of years ago.

That same year, Arnold played a modern hero in the all-out action film *Commando*. Arnold's character was a retired government strike force leader, who was forced out of retirement and back into action when his daughter was kidnapped. He liked doing two very different films in one year, set in two different worlds. It gave his fans a sense of variety within the action genre of movie-making. Arnold especially enjoyed working on *Commando* because he got to work with children, something he loves dearly. Even today, his work with children—teaching about fitness, and volunteering for the Special Olympics—are among the most satisfying of Arnold's off-screen activities.

By 1986, movie offers were pouring in left and right. Arnold was making films almost nonstop. Next up was *Raw Deal*. Shot in Chicago, *Raw Deal* is the story of an ex-FBI agent who is kicked out of the bureau because he used too much violence in his work. On his own, he carries out an investigation and tracks down some gangsters in order to get back in good with the FBI.

Arnold appeared in two major science-fiction action movies in 1987. In *Predator*, he played a special agent in South America who must track down and stop a monster from outer space. Co-starring with Arnold in this sci-fi extravaganza were *Rocky's* Carl Weathers, and professional wrestler Jesse "The Body" Ventura.

Once again Arnold had to endure difficult filming conditions. He had to wear special camouflage makeup, and often found himself covered head to toe in mud. "It was miserable," said Arnold. "I'd go from sweating under the mud and makeup to diving into icy cold water."

Also in 1987, Arnold starred in an unusual science fiction movie called *The Running Man*. This dark vision of the future co-starred Richard Dawson as the host of a futuristic game show on which contestants face gladiator-type battles against a variety of killers armed with everything from buzzsaws to exploding hockey pucks! Arnold plays a good man trying to get by in a violent, evil world.

The Running Man was an important film for Arnold for more than the fact that it was yet another big-grossing action blockbuster. For the first time, Arnold got to deliver some funny lines. His character would throw around wisecracks to relieve the tension of many of the film's scenes. For the first time Arnold's sense of humor came through in a movie. It was an omen of things to come!

In 1988 Arnold worked on a project that was both personally rewarding, as well as historic. *Red Heat* was the film. In it, he plays a Russian policeman who comes to America to investigate a murder. While his role in the movie was nothing unusual, part of the film was shot in Austria, not far from his childhood stamping ground of Graz. It pleased Arnold to be working so close to his home town.

Red Heat was historic because in February of 1988 Arnold and the crew traveled to Moscow in the Soviet Union where they were the first American film crew ever allowed to film in Moscow's Red Square.

Arnold's co-star in *Red Heat* was the *Saturday Night Live* comedian Jim Belushi. "Arnold is a very intelligent actor," said Belushi. "I called him 'The Professor.' Off screen, he did all the talking. He taught me about finance, real estate, and publicity! He's really an amazing guy."

Arnold's work with comedian Belushi in *Red Heat* was yet one more step toward the next phase of his career. He didn't want to always be the tough guy, always be the killer or the cop or the robot. Arnold was ready to make people laugh!

Arnold Schwarzenegger and Danny DeVito in *Twins*.

Chapter 5

THIS GUY IS FUNNY, TOO!

Arnold Schwarzenegger will always remember 1988 as a year of laughs. In March of that year he became part of a 50-year-old Hollywood tradition, when the Friars—an organization of comedians and entertainers—held a roast for Arnold. A roast in Hollywood is a big banquet at which many comedians and celebrities take turns getting up and insulting the person being roasted—in a joking and warm way.

Arnold's roast was the longest in the Friars' history, lasting five hours. Some of the guest roasters were Jesse "The Body" Ventura, Carl Weathers, Danny DeVito, Bruce Willis, James Earl Jones, Milton Berle, Sid Caeser, Henny Youngman, and George Carlin.

Arnold loved being the center of attention, and felt the affection of these great comedians through their friendly put-downs. "I'm such an easy target," says Arnold. "They made fun of my name, my muscles, my accent, my relationship with the Kennedys."

Within a month of the roast, Arnold was hard at work filming his first comedy, *Twins*. "It was a another dream come true," he recalls. "I finally got what I wanted for a long time—a funny role."

With *Twins*, Arnold was working with two of film comedy's top talents. Danny DeVito, his co-star, was the driving force in the hit television series *Taxi* during its long, successful run, and had also starred in many top film comedies. Arnold's director in *Twins*, Ivan Reitman, directed the comedy classics, *Ghostbusters I* and *II*.

Arnold and DeVito played two brothers with different fathers. Arnold's character, Julius Benedict, was scientifically created to have mankind's most perfect traits. The movie was very funny and Arnold was delighted to be working in a comedy. He was thrilled to be able to show audiences another side of the bodybuilding\action hero. He played a far sweeter and more vulnerable character, one that his audience could actually think was lovable. He had always been a natural comedian, and in *Twins* he was able to bring that humor and charm to the big screen for the first time in his career.

"I always knew I had a feel for comedy and a sense of humor," says Arnold. "This made my work in *Twins* much easier."

Twins opened in December of 1988 and was a huge hit. President Bush, a long time Schwarzenegger fan, attended the premiere. Arnold the comedian was on his way!

In 1991, Arnold's comedic dreams reached their peak. In *Kindergarten Cop* he was the solo star in a major film comedy. *Kindergarten Cop* is the story of an undercover cop, played by Arnold, who must go underground to track down some criminals. In order to keep his identity unknown, he must pose as a kindergarten teacher. The cop soon learns that a classroom full of five-year-olds can be more dangerous than a truck load of bad guys.

Arnold loved playing this role. He got to poke fun at the many tough-guy cop roles he had played over the years. He also got to work with kids, something he enjoys dong off screen as well as on. And, of course, he got to be funny.

As much as Arnold loved working on comedies, he was a shrewd enough businessman to realize that action films would always be his bread and butter. During the time he worked on *Twins* and *Kindergarten Cop*, Arnold also made two science fiction action films—films that would prove to be the finest artistically and most successful commercially that he had done so far.

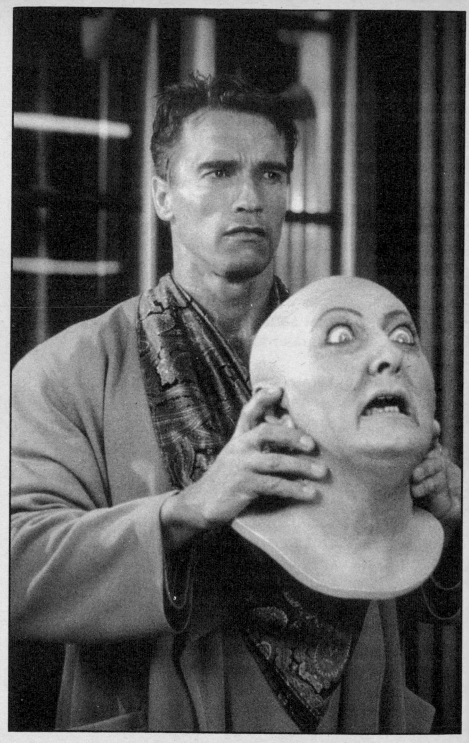

Arnold in *Total Recall*.

Chapter 6

A HERO FOR THE '90S: TOTAL RECALL AND T2

Part of Arnold's genius is that each time he moved in a new career direction, he kept one foot firmly planted in the area that had already brought him success. *Pumping Iron* made him a movie star, but it was a movie about Arnold the bodybuilder.

As much as he was thrilled to finally play comedic roles in *Twins* and *Kindergarten Cop*, he knew better than to abandon his work in action films. Once again, Arnold's instincts were right on the money.

In the movie world, the summer of 1990 was the summer of *Total Recall*. The movie was based on the book entitled "We Can Dream it for you Wholesale," written by Philip K. Dick, one of science fiction's most prestigious writers. This was, by far, the most lofty action film Arnold had ever attempted. Another Philip Dick book had been turned into the sci-fi blockbuster *Blade Runner* in the early 1980s, and Arnold was proud to be associated with a movie based on the work of one of science fiction's most respected authors.

Total Recall was indeed the monster hit of 1990, and Arnold was never better. Set on Earth in the future, Arnold plays a man who dreams of going to Mars. He meets up with people who can actually plant dreams in your head, so that it feels as if you have been to some exotic place, when in reality, you have never even left your seat! When Arnold finally does get to Mars, Arnold's character leads a revolt to free a colony of enslaved workers.

This movie also allowed Arnold to use his sense of humor. In between action scenes there was always time for a gag line that fit right into Arnold's character. In addition, the special effects in *Total Recall* were astounding, and they combined with Arnold's appeal to make for a huge blockbuster.

Arnold's control over his career also grew with this film. He had the right to approve of the script, cast, and advertising associated with *Total Recall*. Using this power, Arnold was able to tailor the project to firmly establish himself as the king of the action movies, and as America's superstar hero of the 90s.

Arnold came right back the following year with that summer's number one action extravaganza, *Terminator 2: Judgement Day*, the sequel to the 1984 hit that really established him as a legitimate action star.

T2, as the film came to be know, once again showed audiences Arnold's versatility. In the original *Terminator* movie Arnold played a vicious robot. He was a machine from the future sent back in time to kill a woman who would one day give birth to a very important leader. In *T2* the robot that Arnold plays is reprogrammed to protect this same woman, played in both films by TV's *Beauty and the Beast* star Linda Hamilton, from a more advanced and deadly Terminator, sent back to finish the job that Arnold had begun in the original film. Whether he was playing the good guy or the bad guy, Arnold's persona was so strong that audiences found themselves rooting for him in both films.

Linda Hamilton worked out for her role in *T2* and she recalls what a help Arnold was. "My character needed to be pretty pumped up. Although Arnold and I each had our own separate training facilities, he was always happy to answer any questions I had about fitness and training. He was great to work with both on and off the set."

T2 had one of the highest budgets in the history of filmmaking, and also broke new ground in special effects and computer animation tech-

The Terminator and *Terminator 2* are super hits!

niques. The new model Terminator in the second film was made of liquid metal and could reshape itself into any form. The stunning effect of seeing this transformation on the screen left movie audiences gasping in amazement!

Arnold Schwarzenegger seems to have everything going for him professionally. But what about his personal life?

There too, Arnold is a winner.

Arnold with his beautiful wife, Maria Shriver.

Chapter 7

ARNOLD AND MARIA

When Arnold Schwarzenegger met Maria
Shriver at the Robert F. Kennedy Tennis
Tournament in Forest Hills, New York in August of
1977, there was an instant attraction. Arnold
thought Maria was smart, pretty, and funny.
Maria thought Arnold was bright and very handsome. They were both right.

When Maria invited Arnold to visit her at
the Kennedy family vacation home in
Hyannisport, Massachusetts, he was a bit ner-
vous. He had come from such a poor back-
ground, and she was part of one of the most
famous families in history.

Much to Arnold's surprise, he had a terrif-
ic time. He went boating with Maria's mom, and

played tennis with her dad. Following that visit, Arnold and Maria started dating regularly. Their biggest problem was that they lived on opposite coasts. Arnold was in Hollywood making movies, and Maria was on the east coast, working in TV news. She worked first in Baltimore and Philadelphia, then in New York, for CBS-TV News.

Crosscountry airplane flights kept their romance alive. Many people were surprised when Arnold and Maria ended up falling in love. No one was more surprised than Arnold himself! "When I first came to this country from Europe, my image of the ideal wife was someone like my mother. She was a woman who stayed at home, cooked and cleaned for her husband, and never went to work outside of the house. But after spending some time here I came to appreciate women who were independent, and had their own careers. Maria is just that kind of woman."

The happy couple didn't rush right into marriage. In fact they dated for eight years before they even got engaged. "I carried the engagement ring around with me for half a year," said Arnold. "I could never seem to find the right place to pop the question."

Then Arnold had an idea. In August of 1985 he invited Maria to journey to Austria with him. He was very excited to show her his home town, so she could find out more about his childhood. Once in

Austria, Arnold took Maria boating. Right there in the middle of the Thalersee River, in Arnold's home town, he asked Maria to marry him. "It was the most romantic day of my life," Arnold remembers.

The wedding was set for April 26, 1986. Making all the arrangements proved to be a tough task. Maria was working on a morning TV news show in New York, while Arnold was flying back and forth between Hollywood sound stages and a location in Mexico, for the film *Predator.*

Finally, wedding plans were made. The reception would be held at the Kennedy home in Hyannisport. Maria's mom and her cousin, Caroline Kennedy helped with the details of the parties. And what parties they were!

The celebration started on Friday afternoon, April 25, the day before the wedding. Caroline Kennedy threw a clam chowder lunch for the couple and their guests. That night an Austrian clambake was held. Arnold wore a traditional Austrian costume for this party.

The next day, reporters and photographers began to gather at the church at 6 am—five hours before the wedding! Caroline Kennedy was Maria's maid of honor, and Franco Columbu, an old body-building pal and business partner of Arnold's was the best man.

After the ceremony, a huge party was held at the Kennedy house, after which the newlyweds left for their honeymoon in Antigua.

During the first few years of marriage, Arnold and Maria still lived on opposite coasts and couldn't see as much of each other as they would have liked. In 1989, all that changed. Maria moved to the couple's house in California, and the couple settled down and decided to have a family.

On December 13, 1989 Katherine Eunice Schwarzenegger was born, and Arnold's life was changed forever. Then in the spring of 1991, they had a second child, Christina Maria Aurelia. "I love being a dad," says Arnold. "For me, it's the greatest thrill of all!"

These days Arnold and Maria spend lots of time at home with Katherine and Christina. Arnold's office is close to their home, and he travels less for his movies. He is indeed a happy man.

Chapter 8

A COMMITMENT TO FITNESS

Bodybuilding was the key that led to Arnold's tremendous success, but his feeling for fitness has always gone much deeper than simply a career. "I learned as a student in Austria that involvement in physical activity always made me feel good," he recalls. "Even before I technically understood why, I always felt my best after a workout."

Even though it's been years since he has competed professionally as a bodybuilder, Arnold still loves going to the gym every day. "Everyone can benefit from fitness," believes Arnold. "Young and old alike."

As with everything else in his life, Arnold backs up his words and beliefs with action. He travels around the country promoting fitness. He has visited prisons, where he has talked to inmates about how getting in shape can make them feel better about themselves.

For over a decade, Arnold has worked with the Special Olympics. He acts as the weight training coach and also raises money for this important organization—started over 20 years ago by Maria's mother—that allows retarded and handicapped kids to compete in athletic events.

Perhaps Arnold's greatest honor in fitness came when President Bush named him chairman of the President's Council on Physical Fitness and Sports. Arnold has promised to use his position as chairman to help make the 1990s "The Fitness Decade."

If being named chairman of the President's Council was Arnold's greatest honor, his greatest thrill remains talking to kids about fitness. He is concerned that American kids are not in as good shape as they could be. To help remedy this, Arnold travels tirelessly from state to state, meeting with young people and talking at schools.

During a visit to one school in Virginia, Arnold spent over an hour working with fourth-grade students. He climbed ropes, bounced on a trampoline, jumped rope, and lifted weights with the kids. He also showed them the proper way to do push-ups, sit-ups, and stretching exercises.

Arnold is upset by the fact that most schools in America don't have gym class every day. This is something he very badly wants to change. "I want to make fitness hip for kids," he explains. "I want to challenge kids to work out every day, to get involved in sports, and to stay away from drugs and junk food. I also believe that families should exercise together, simple things like taking a walk after dinner, playing catch, riding bikes. There are a hundred simple ways to stay in shape."

Arnold's fitness lessons even extend to the White House. In 1990, Arnold launched the first Great American Workout. It took place on the White House lawn. Arnold got a group of famous athletes together for a day of teaching, fitness demonstrations, and exercise. Some of the celebrity athletes included Jackie Joyner-Kersee, Eric Dickerson, Dominique Wilkins, Carl Lewis, and Mary Lou Retton.

As far as the future goes, Arnold plans to continue traveling around the country, promoting fitness, and to keep making action and comedy movies. And that's certainly good news for his millions of loyal fans around the world!

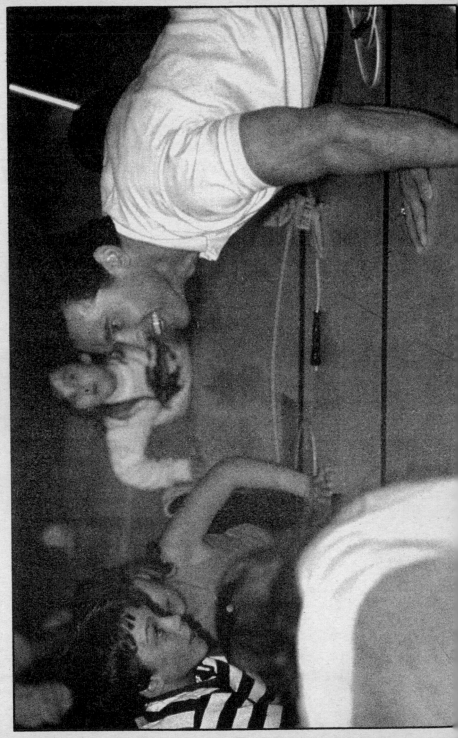

Working out with kids is one of Arnold's greatest pleasures

Chapter 9

STATS & FACTS & QUOTES & FLICKS

Arnold Schwarzenegger
Birthdate: July 30, 1947
Birthplace: Thal, Austria
Height: 6' 2"
Weight: His weight has been as low as 200 pounds and as high as 250. He averages around 210-215.
Typical Menu During Bodybuilding:
Breakfast: Three scrambled eggs, coffee
Lunch: One hamburger, a serving of chicken or fish, a can of tuna with eggs and mayo
Dinner: Large sirloin steak, salad, hot chocolate
Bodybuilding Titles:
Seven Mr. Olympias, **five** Mr. Universes, **one** Mr. World
Shoe size: 12
Shirt size: Extra, extra large
Amount lifted during training day: 50 tons

Amount lifted with legs in one lift: 600 pounds
Amount lifted while standing straight: 200 pounds
Measurements during peak of bodybuilding competitions: chest: 67", biceps: 22", waist: 31", thighs: 22", calves: 20"
Salary for first movie: $1,000 per week
Current salary per movie: $15 million
Books written: "Arnold: The Education of a Bodybuilder"; "Arnold's Bodyshaping for Women"; "Arnold's Bodybuilding for Men"; Arnold's Encyclopedia of Modern Bodybuilding"
Favorite sports: Bodybuilding, running, skiing, river rafting, horseback riding
Favorite hobby: Art collecting, talking about fitness

Quoting Arnold:

"As a boy, I was looking for something I could be a champion in."

"Strength does not come from winning. Your struggles develop your strength. When you go through hardships and decide not to surrender, that is strength."

"I have a tremendous joy when I go to the gym."

"We all have great inner power. The power is self-faith. You have to see yourself winning before you even start to compete."

"The people in Hollywood had many reasons why they thought I would never make it: my accent, my body, my name. I just didn't listen to them."

"Good things don't happen by coincidence. Every dream carries with it certain risks, especially the risk of failure. If you take the risk and fail, you must try again and again."

"My goal is to make fitness hip."

"I knew that Maria was the woman for me, and she has been the greatest addition to my life and my happiness. Looking back, I can say that every year I've been with her I've loved her more."

Schwarzenegger on Screen:

1970 - *Hercules Goes Bananas*
1974 - *The Long Good-bye*
1976 - *Stay Hungry*
1977 - *Pumping Iron*
1979 - *The Villain*
1979 - *The Jayne Mansfield Story*
1979 - *The Scavenger Hunt*
1982 - *Conan the Barbarian*
1984 - *Conan the Destroyer*
1984 - *The Terminator*
1985 - *Red Sonja*
1985 - *Commando*
1986 - *Raw Deal*
1987 - *Predator*
1987 - *The Running Man*
1988 - *Red Heat*
1988 - *Twins*
1990 - *Total Recall*
1991 - *Kindergarten Cop*
1991 - *Terminator 2: Judgement Day*

Kindergarten Cop is a smash with children and adults.

Chapter 10

THE OFFICIAL ARNOLD SCHWARZENEGGER TRIVIA QUIZ

Test your Schwarzenegger I.Q. with this trivia quiz:

1) Arnold was born in what country?
2) In what city?
3) What was Arnold's father's name?
4) What was his father's profession?
5) What was his father's hobby?
6) In what year did Arnold win his first Mr. Universe contest?
7) How old was he when he won?
8) What character did Arnold play in his first movie?
9) What was the name of the bodybuilding movie that brought Arnold to the spotlight?
10) Who directed *Conan the Barbarian*?

Multiple Choice

11) Arnold was part of the first film crew to ever film in: a) Times Square, b) Harvard Square, c) Red Square, d) Hollywood Squares

12) The director of *Twins* was:
a) Bill Murray, b) Ivan Reitman, c) Dino De Laurentiis, d) Robert Altman

13) The Kennedy summer home is in: a) Hyannisport, b) Williamsport, c) Port Jervis, d) Port Washington

14) Arnold's brother's name was: a) Kurt, b) Meinike, c) Carl, d) Meinhard

15) When Arnold was a kid, he met film star: a) Clark Gable, b) Steve Reeves, c) Johnny Weismuller, d) Marilyn Monroe

16) In order to train, Arnold moved from Austria to: a) Hungary, b) Germany, c) India, d) Canada

17) Arnold and Maria met in: a) Austria, b) California, c) Cape Cod, d) Forest Hills

18) In *Total Recall*, Arnold travels to: a) Mars, b) Venus, c) Jupiter, d) New Jersey

19) The biggest city near Arnold's home town of Thal was: a) Matz, b) Graz, c) Budapest, d) New York

20) The TV comedienne who put Arnold on her special was: a) Carol Burnett, b) Bea Arthur, c) Lucille Ball, d) Betty White

Fill in the Blanks

21) Arnold's mother's name is _____.
22) In Austria, Arnold was a junior champion in the sport of _____.
23) In his first movie, Arnold used the last name _____.
24) The authors of "Pumping Iron" were _____ and _____.
25) Arnold became a U.S. citizen in _____.
26) The maid of honor at Arnold and Maria's wedding was _____.
27) The best man was _____.
28) Arnold and Maria's daughters' names are _____ and _____.
29) In *Raw Deal* Arnold played a member of the _____.
30) In *Predator* Arnold worked with _____ and _____.

True or False

31) Bob Rafelson directed *Stay Hungry*.
32) Arnold was older than his brother.
33) Bodybuilding began in the 1950s.
34) Arnold's mother was at the premiere of *Pumping Iron*.
35) Arnold wore a red, white, and blue suit the day he became a citizen.
36) Arnold and Maria got married in 1986.
37) Arnold is chairman of the president's council of movie making.

38) Arnold wears a size 14 shoe.

39) Arnold has written four books.

40) Arnold played the good guy in *T2*.

Schwarzenegger Matching Quiz

Match each of these Schwarzenegger co-stars with the movie in which they appeared:

41) Linda Hamilton	a) *Red Sonja*
42) Danny DeVito	b) *Red Heat*
43) Jim Belushi	c) *The Terminator*
44) Brigitte Nielsen	d) *Conan the Barbarian*
45) Sandahl Bergman	e) *Twins*

Answers

1) Austria, 2) Thal, 3) Gustav, 4) chief of police, 5) playing music, 6) 1967, 7) 20, 8) Hercules, 9) *Pumping Iron*, 10) John Milius, 11) c, 12) b, 13) a, 14) d, 15) c, 16) b, 17) d, 18) a, 19) b, 20) c, 21) Aurelia, 22) Ice Curling, 23) Strong, 24) Charles Gaines, George Butler, 25) 1983, 26) Caroline Kennedy, 27) Franco Columbu, 28) Katherine, Christina, 29) FBI, 30) Carl Weathers, Jesse "The Body" Ventura, 31) True, 32) False, 33) False, 34) True, 35) True, 36) True, 37) False, 38) False, 39) True, 40) True, 41) c, 42) e, 43) b, 44) a, 45) d